# 100 Day Tear-Off Countdown Calendar

Transcripture International

100 Day Tear-Off Countdown Calendar

ISBN-13: 978-1922217547

Published by Transcripture International.

For inquiries and bulk orders please visit http://www.buycountdowncalendar.com/

20131204065411-100-P

# How to Use This Calendar

## Step 1: Decide How to Hang

This calendar is best viewed when hung on a wall. Below are some suggested hanging methods:

1) Make holes through the two outermost guide marks on the cover near the binding and hang the calendar with string.
2) Make a hole through the middle guide mark on the cover and hang on a nail or screw.
3) Push thumb tacks through the back cover to attach the calendar to a pin board
4) Glue the back cover to a larger piece of cardboard that can be attached to or hung on a wall.

## Step 2: Prepare for Hanging

Remove the front cover and the first two pages, including this page, to expose the first day.

The last page of this calendar is blank so you can remove the last printed page and display something else such as a special message or photograph instead if you wish.

## Step 3: Start the Countdown!

Hang the calendar as desired then, as each day passes, remove one page by tearing along the marked guidelines using a ruler or scissors. Pages can also be removed by carefully tearing along the binding.

# 100

**DAYS LEFT**

# 99

DAYS LEFT

98

DAYS LEFT

# 97

**DAYS LEFT**

# 96

DAYS LEFT

# 95

**DAYS LEFT**

# 94

**DAYS LEFT**

# 93

## DAYS LEFT

# 92

# DAYS LEFT

# 19

## DAYS LEFT

# 90

**DAYS LEFT**

98

DAYS LEFT

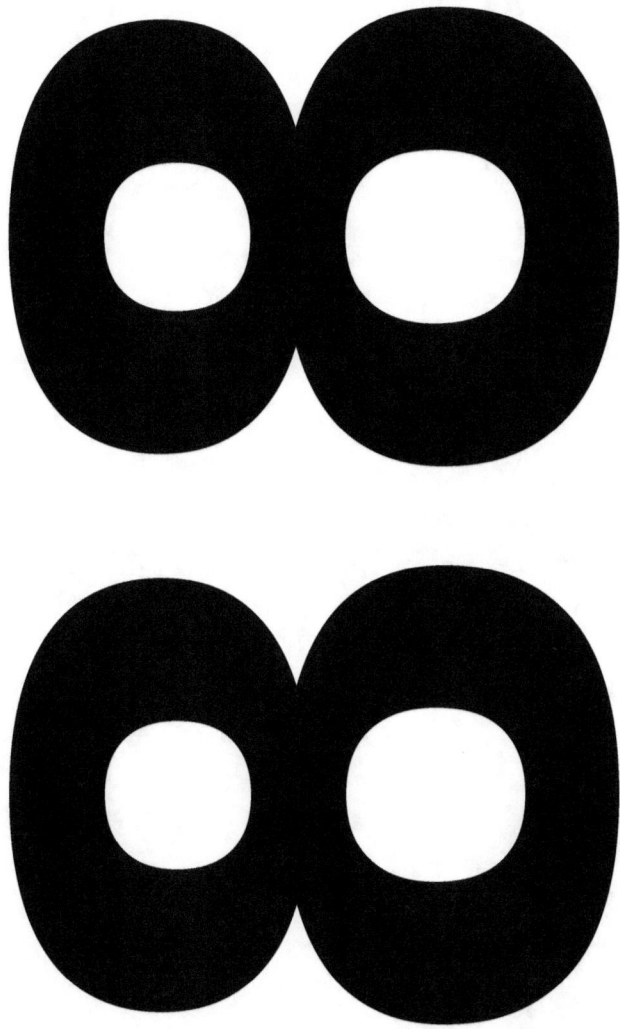

# 88

**DAYS LEFT**

78

DAYS LEFT

# 68

**DAYS LEFT**

58

DAYS LEFT

# 48

**DAYS LEFT**

38

DAYS LEFT

# 28

DAYS LEFT

**18 DAYS LEFT**

# 80

**DAYS LEFT**

# 9

DAYS LEFT

# 8

# 7

DAYS LEFT

# 11

**DAYS LEFT**

# 76

DAYS LEFT

# 72

**DAYS LEFT**

14

DAYS LEFT

# 3

DAYS LEFT

# 2

**DAYS LEFT**

# 71

**DAYS LEFT**

# 70

## DAYS LEFT

# 69

DAYS LEFT

# 68

# 60

DAYS LEFT

# 76

**DAYS LEFT**

# 60

**DAYS LEFT**

**56**

**DAYS LEFT**

64

DAYS LEFT

# 30

**DAYS LEFT**

# 269

## DAYS LEFT

# 16 DAYS LEFT

# 60

DAYS LEFT

95

DAYS LEFT

# 85

DAYS LEFT

# 15 DAYS LEFT

# 95

## DAYS LEFT

55

DAYS LEFT

# 54

**DAYS LEFT**

# 3
# 5
# DAYS LEFT

25

DAYS LEFT

# 15

## DAYS LEFT

50

DAYS LEFT

# 49

**DAYS LEFT**

84

DAYS LEFT

74

DAYS LEFT

64

DAYS LEFT

# 115

DAYS LEFT

44

DAYS LEFT

# 34

DAYS LEFT

# 24

## DAYS LEFT

14

DAYS LEFT

# 40

DAYS LEFT

# 39

**DAYS LEFT**

# 30

**DAYS LEFT**

# 131

**DAYS LEFT**

30 DAYS LEFT

# 35

DAYS LEFT

# 34

DAYS LEFT

# 3

# DAYS LEFT

23 DAYS LEFT

# 13 DAYS LEFT

# 30

## DAYS LEFT

# 92

DAYS LEFT

82

DAYS LEFT

# 12

**DAYS LEFT**

# 26

## DAYS LEFT

52

DAYS LEFT

# 24

## DAYS LEFT

# 32

## DAYS LEFT

# 2 DAYS LEFT

12 DAYS LEFT

# 20

## DAYS LEFT

19

DAYS LEFT

# 18

DAYS LEFT

# 1

DAYS LEFT

16

DAYS LEFT

15 DAYS LEFT

# 14

DAYS LEFT

# 13

**DAYS LEFT**

# 21

## DAYS LEFT

# 11

**DAYS LEFT**

# 10

## DAYS LEFT

9

DAYS LEFT

8

DAYS LEFT

# 7

**DAYS LEFT**

6 DAYS LEFT

5

DAYS LEFT

# 4

**DAYS LEFT**

3 DAYS LEFT

# 2

DAYS LEFT

1 DAY LEFT

O DAYS LEFT

www.ingramcontent.com/pod-product-compliance
Lightning Source LLC
LaVergne TN
LVHW081315060426
835509LV00015B/1530